Yves Saint Laurent with a model from the fall/winter collection of 1983–84, the famous long evening dress of black velvet and pink satin, "Paris." Photo by David Bailey.

YVES SAINT LAURENT

IMAGES OF DESIGN
1958-1988

with an introduction by
Marguerite Duras

EBURY PRESS
LONDON

Published by Ebury Press
Division of The National Magazine Company Ltd
Colquhoun House
27–37 Broadwick Street
LONDON W1V 1FR

First impression 1988
Copyright © 1988 by Schirmer/Mosel
Introduction copyright © 1988 by Marguerite Duras
A Schirmer/Mosel production

ISBN 0 85223 771 5

Manufactured in the Federal Republic of Germany

Acknowledgments

We would like to thank Yves Saint Laurent and Pierre Bergé
for making this book possible.

Our special thanks go to Marguerite Duras
and all contributing photographers.

We are also grateful to the staff of the
Yves Saint Laurent maison,
especially Isabelle de Courrèges and Gabrielle Buchaert,
who contributed to this book
with their work and friendly helpfulness.

Many people around the world have given us their friendly
support in manifold ways or were
instrumental in acquiring the photos.
In Paris we thank:
Ute Mundt, Jackie Fixot, Martine Mollard, Björn Amelan,
Dominique Genet, Alain Lopez, and Philippe Serieys;
in New York:
Diane Edkins, Shelley Dowell, Betty Klarnet, Pam Reid, and Patricia McCabe;
in London:
Lillie Davis, Sara Preston, Alex Kroll,
Robin Muir, and Peter Lyster-Todd;
in Milan:
Marina Taroni, Davide Manfredi, and Franco Sartori;
in Munich:
Helga Margaret Colle-Tietz, Felicitas Oeltze von Lobenthal,
and Thomas Elsner.

Our special thanks go to Anne de Margerie, Paris,
who inspired the project
and promoted and supervised it from the beginning
to its happy end.
Without her energy and vigilant enthusiasm
this book could never have
come about in its existing form.

The Photographers

Richard Avedon
David Bailey
Gian Paolo Barbieri
Neal Barr
Roland Bianchini
Pierre Boulat
Guy Bourdin
Alex Chatelain
Richard Dormer
Arthur Elgort
Fouli Elia
Hans Feurer
Antonio Guccione
Rodolphe Haussaire
Hiro
Horst P. Horst
Frank Horvat
Dominique Issermann
William Klein
Tom Kublin
François Lamy
Barry Lategan
Peter Lindbergh

Manuel Litran
Roxanne Lowit
Duane Michals
Sarah Moon
Helmut Newton
Norman Parkinson
Irving Penn
Denis Piel
Bettina Rheims
Willy Rizzo
Franco Rubartelli
Sacha
Jean-Claude Sauer
Francesco Scavullo
Lothar Schmid
Paul Schutzer
Seeberger
David Seidner
Jeanloup Sieff
Snowdon
Melvin Sokolsky
Bert Stern
Gilles Tapie

Bruce Weber

The Sound and the Silence

He is childlike. He is tall. Alto. A man from Oran with white skin. One day they came into the great hall of the Rond-Point during a *Savannah Bay* rehearsal, Pierre Bergé and he. We heard nothing — neither the door nor the footsteps. Suddenly they were there, two meters away from us. They were silent, discreet, but their presence was of kings.

I know him only slightly. We've spoken two or three times, of theater dresses, colors, fabrics, of the deep red velvet of a certain gown. Once he talked of my books.

He's an intimidating man, more so, surely, than most — more so than any doctor or actor you will meet. Yet he's shy and vulnerable, too.

He looms up, putting his face with its naked, inscrutable smile close to yours — and nothing in that look suggests the power of the man. There is no hint of pretense or play-acting. One is simply overwhelmed. It is too much all at once, this bodily presence.

The look on Yves Saint Laurent's face cannot be described. It is unbearably sweet and sad, yet in its quality of infinite solitude it can make itself masterful.

He sees in you what you cannot see: your own mortality. This is the point where all begins for the man from Oran.

That look! He *looks* at what he sees, and (like all the world) sees with eyes open, just as he sees with eyes closed — around him, near him, far and beyond. Only observe the result.

I cannot but believe that for Yves Saint Laurent the act of creation is a sort of sleep — blinding, deathly, dark; it is the night of the body. Call it a void — the soul of inspiration. When in photographs or on television I see Yves Saint Laurent smile, talk to famous people, I tell myself: "Voilà! They've woken him again."

I will always see him as a writer. His work is not of words, yet I think of it as of the written word; for where the intellect is finest-tuned, silent, it sets itself to writing. He finds in each one of us a whole world to embrace.

The whole of life, or life's detail — it's all one to Yves Saint Laurent: a crowd, a man, a throng, a desert, a person before him, an empty set. Like a writer, each day is as the first. Like the text which owes its meaning to a single comma, his world hangs by a comma also; done, undone, to be re-begun.

Let me explain again: he sees each of us as part of an "everyone" — the lost one, drowned by the many. "But," you will tell me, "we all see ourselves and others thus...." Yes, that's it.

He sees in you what you don't know you have. What you thought you had he doesn't look at, because you don't have it. You never had it. He takes you apart. He reaffirms your mortality. You feel nothing, you let it happen, because in his relationship with you, in the course of this exchange that he is orchestrating between you and yourself, you are going through a sacrificial process. He and you. He distorts your bodily self. You thought you were not beautiful, yet from your very longing to be so, he draws a new beauty. This is your transformation for eternity.

There is a woman, he is here. He draws, and there is the woman — dressed.

I tend to believe that the fabulous universality of Yves Saint Laurent comes from a religious disposition toward garnering the real, be it man-made — the temples of the Nile — or not man-made — the forest of Telemark, the floor of the ocean, or apple trees in bloom. Yves Saint Laurent invents a reality and adds it to the other, the one he has not made. And he fuses all of this in a paradoxical harmony — often revolutionary, always dazzling. Yes, this is it; he makes dazzling explosions of stuff.

He makes a dress. He puts a woman in that dress in the middle of desert sands, and it is as though the desert had been waiting for that dress. The dress was what the desert demanded — it speaks volumes.

When a dress of Yves Saint Laurent's appears in a salon, or on television, we cry with joy. For the dress we had never dreamed of is there, and it is just the one we were waiting for, and just that year. We are the desert that was waiting for the dress, and thus each day we wait for the moment of truth.

To put it another way, it's incredible to be *recognized* to this degree by the entire world, including those who will never have access to Yves Saint Laurent's clothes. Year after year he creates what we knew (though we didn't know we knew it) that we wanted. Imagine!

The price of a dress has nothing to do with the dress itself (nor has the price of a painting to do with the painting — remember how the theft of Monet's *Rising Sun* cut to the quick?). With prêt-à-porter, elitism in high fashion is no longer an issue. Yves Saint Laurent women are made in the harem, the château, on the edges of cities . . . they are in the streets, the Métro, Prisunic, the Bourse.

As for Yves Saint Laurent himself, it would seem that the adoration of which he is the object is of no importance to him — it is, after all, nothing to do with him (I hear him say). What is hardest of all to put into words is his attitude of self-disregard. He's one of those people who are attracted by the sublimation of the self, drawn to the annihilation of that certain part of the self which they themselves do not name, but others call life. More than that I will not say — it cannot be expressed.

The look again: it's his — uniquely, absolutely his (and that's not lightly said). He sees a woman, a man, a garden, a prison, the ocean, a photograph of Auschwitz, the laughter of a child: no analysis, no reflection on these things that touch his life so closely. He does not speak of good and bad. The particular and the general — it's all one to him; he embraces the whole with its good and its bad, or he leaves the whole aside. And I think that he's right (though he may not *know* he is right) to gather it all up or leave it all behind. Humanity must take upon itself every crime, every smile. All must be assumed. Without this — no writer. No Yves Saint Laurent.

It is like a road. From the night of the intellect comes forth a road, and to start the journey down that road one word is needed, or two: "hips," let us say, and "strut." Then the hips sway into motion along the road and the rest comes after: legs, arms, the top of the body — they rise out of those sinuous hips swathed in pink, the rest black or a wild blue or a secret red they call amarante, from Cayenne, like the flowers of the same name, like people, like Rimbaud, like Mozart.

Sometimes I call Yves Saint Laurent by the name of another man. It happens in winter, at night, there is snow, and from behind a wall, and across time, someone who is not sleeping composes music to be sung.

Marguerite Duras, Summer 1987

Plates

*Yves Saint Laurent is a shy young man of twenty-one when, in 1957, he is named successor
to the legendary Parisian fashion creator Christian Dior. It is the beginning of a momentous
career in which the novice, praised as child prodigy, makes it as "king of the couturiers," the
most celebrated and influential fashion designer of our time. Photo by Irving Penn, 1957.*

Stage fright: Yves Saint Laurent sneaks a look at the premiere audience. He is at the turning point of his career. In the fall of 1961, Dior's successor became independent and together with his friend Pierre Bergé established his own maison de couture. January 29, 1962, was the premiere, with an opening spring/summer collection of one hundred models. The applause was tumultuous and the success immediate. Photo by Pierre Boulat.

"Art is probably too big a word for fashion. Fashion is a craft, a poetic craft...." This maxim of Yves Saint Laurent's was convincingly illustrated by the suits of his first collection — this is a cowboy-look model of red-black tweed with a silk bowed blouse and matching hat. Photo by Paul Schutzer.

A daytime ensemble from the spring/summer collection of 1962. A marine blue jersey skirt with a so-called Norman frock of white wool-ratiné. The climax of the collection was the headdresses: silk scarves draped over a straw pillbox and tied like a turban at the nape or like a kerchief below the chin. They were dubbed "babushkas" by the American press because of their Russian charm. Photo by Tom Kublin.

A violet silk-tweed afternoon dress from the spring/summer collection of 1962. Photo by William Klein, one of the most prominent fashion photographers of the sixties, who reported on the memorable Yves Saint Laurent debut for American Vogue.

An Yves Saint Laurent classic from the very start: the small afternoon suit, here in gray and white plaid wool with an olive shantung blouse, from the first collection. Photo by William Klein.

*Zizi Jeanmaire was the first to congratulate Saint Laurent after the memorable premiere.
The delicate dancer is his friend, model, and muse. She wears his creations not only in her
private life but also onstage. Saint Laurent has worked countless times for Zizi Jeanmaire
and choreographer Roland Petit, her husband, as costume artist. This photo by Paul Schutzer
appeared in* Life *magazine.*

"The best suits since Chanel," commented Life *on the first collection. This praise spurred him
on: suits have become the trademark of his style and his success; they stand for the inimitable
Yves Saint Laurent mix of perfection, elegance, and wearability. This is a red wool double-
breasted suit with a marine blue shantung blouse. Photo by William Klein.*

*Tout Paris and the crème of the international fashion press are the kingmakers of French
fashion. They all came to the collection premiere on January 29, 1962, at the Forain-Palais
in rue Spontini, where Yves Saint Laurent established himself. And they were all enraptured
by the talent of the new heir to the throne of Parisian haute couture. Photo by Pierre Boulat.*

*Hiro is the first Japanese fashion photographer to have made it to stardom. Born in Beijing,
at home in New York, he began his career at almost the same time as Yves Saint
Laurent, whose models he photographed for all the big fashion magazines. Hiro likes to shoot
from a low angle, a perspective that impressively accentuates both the clear
silhouette of the Saint Laurent suit — like this model in cream-colored silk shantung (spring/
summer of 1962) — and its perfect construction.*

The first collection already displays Yves Saint Laurent's attraction for the splendor of Far Eastern apparel. This white afternoon ensemble of silk-matelassé and crêpe gaufré is reminiscent of the robes of Indian maharajas. The ornate turban is a Saint Laurent headdress that recurs in many of his collections. Pierre Boulat photographed Victoire during the premiere.

Hiro photographed the same model for Harper's Bazaar *at his studio.*

The elegant afternoon dress is the highlight of the spring/summer collection of 1963.
This marine blue wool model with a white organza collar is especially
simple and delicate. Photo by Helmut Newton.

The fall/winter collection of 1963—64 is derived from this black and white plaid
tweed variation with a linen collar. Photo by Richard Dormer.

1962: Yves Saint Laurent was one of the first to recognize the influence of the street and young people. As early as his Dior period, he startled the haute couture patronage with rocker-style, black leather blousons. In the second collection, presented in his own salon, the model wore a black satin-ciré trench-coat with a white evening dress. Photo by Richard Dormer.

This yellow-black napped-tweed ensemble with brown suede trim also comes from the fall/winter collection of 1962–63. Photo by Richard Dormer.

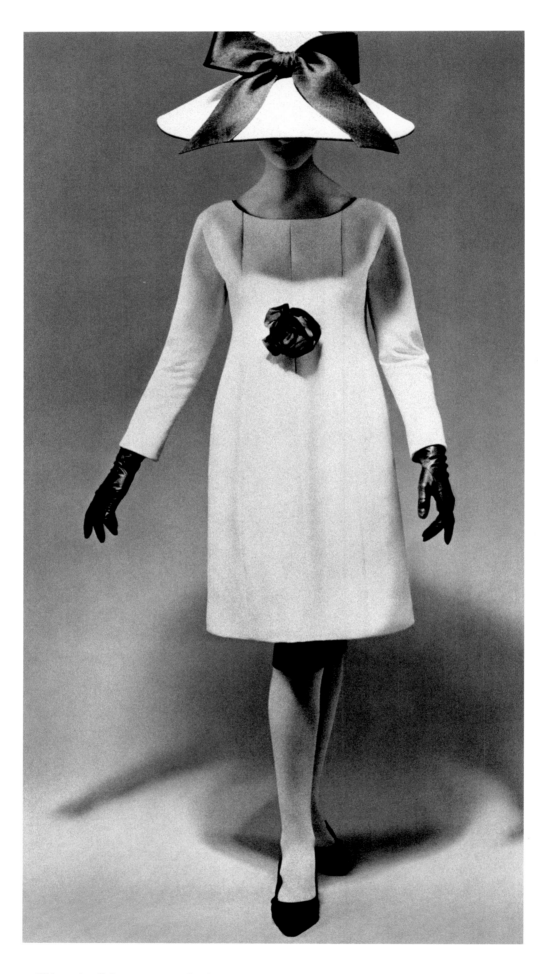

This cocktail dress, a natural-colored shantung, from the spring/summer collection of 1964, was worn by Princess Grace of Monaco. Photo by Seeberger.

Black on black for the Grand Entrance: an evening gown of ciré satin, luxuriously trimmed in lustrous jet. Irving Penn photographed this model from the fall/winter collection of 1962–63 for American Vogue.

34

From the very beginning, the Parisian coiffeur Alexandre supervised the couture showings
of Yves Saint Laurent. This is a selection of chignons with which the exceedingly
elaborate hairstyles of the fall/winter collection of 1962–63 were created.
Photo by Irving Penn.

This photo is something like an artistic summit conference. Audrey Hepburn is wearing an extravagant cape of silk flowers over a classic off-the-shoulder black velvet sheath — a model from the fall/winter collection of 1962–63 — and a hairstyle with chignon by Alexandre. Richard Avedon did the photo for Harper's Bazaar.

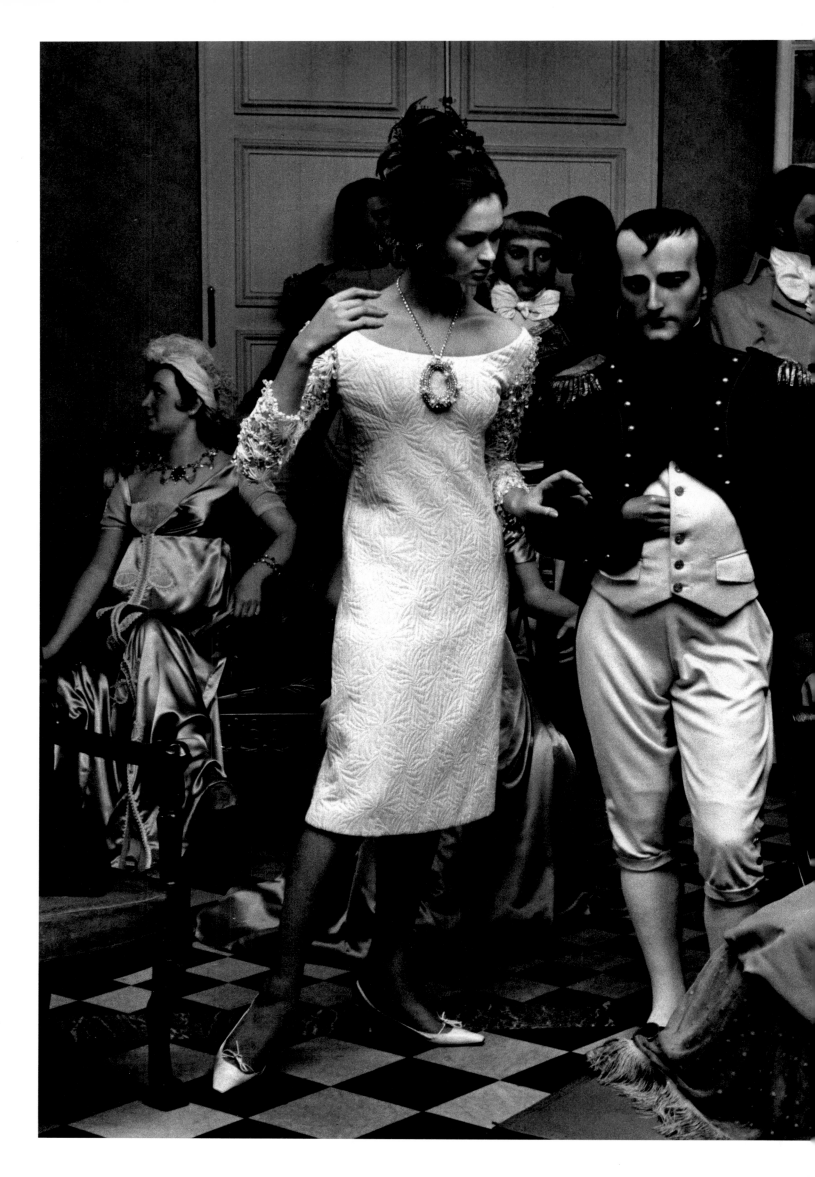

A guest of Napoleon and Josephine in the château of Malmaison. The American photographer William Klein sets up fashion photographs cinematically. When Saint Laurent showed Empire-style apparel in his spring/summer collection of 1963, he staged a retrospective look at history in the wax museum in the Musée Grévin. High-waisted clothing — like this white piqué with guipure-stitched sleeves worn by the only living guest at this evening party frozen at about 1800 — was fashionable at the court of Napoleon I. It has gone down in the history of fashion as the Directoire style or Empire line.

For spring/summer of 1963 Yves Saint Laurent designed this cocktail dress of sand-colored silk shantung and black surah. Photo by Melvin Sokolsky.

The gem of the spring/summer collection of 1964 inspired by Goya: a beige silk shantung evening gown with a tulle tunic trimmed with "emeralds" and fabric blossoms. A green satin ribbon is tied in a decorative bow above the breast — a motif that recurs later in many styles with diverting playfulness. Photo by William Klein.

A daytime ensemble of salmon tweed from the spring/summer collection of 1963. The picture of a perfectly clothed beauty in the middle of a gray, faceless crowd, shot with an alienated effect by William Klein, was considered one of the most impressive photos of this period.

"Robin Hood" was the name of the collection in which Saint Laurent showed leather caps and thigh-high boots for the winter of 1963–64. This caused a big stir, because such young and sporty accessories had not existed among the elitist guild of luxury tailors until then. The American star-photographer Irving Penn gave the Robin Hood helmet a futuristic look.

Jean Shrimpton is wearing one of the most sensational creations of the fall/winter collection of 1965—66, a two-piece evening suit in "page boy" style with pink velvet knee-high breeches and a white lace collar. The prototype was Little Lord Fauntleroy. Yves Saint Laurent is considered the inventor of the pants suit, which became surprisingly popular in women's fashion. The buckled shoes were designed by Roger Vivier, the most famous of French shoe designers. Photo by Guy Bourdin.

The basic idea developed out of a white wool knit cap with a matching turtleneck that Saint Laurent designed for his fall/winter collection of 1960–61, while still at Dior. It was labeled the "Toni Sailor" look at that time. Photo by Irving Penn.

The wedding dress is the solemn finale of each fashion show. Yves Saint Laurent masters this chapter in haute couture with wit and irony. His wedding dress creations have an ingenious and equally fantastic surprise effect every time. In the fall/winter collection of 1965–66, he "entangled" the bride in a white cocoon which he garnished with splendid satin bows. Photo by Fouli Elia.

The "Mondrian" dresses were the sensation of the Paris fashion winter of 1965–66.
Saint Laurent boldly had the paintings of the Dutch constructivist transferred to formless
jersey dresses. In this year the young fashion designer began a serious involvement with
art that was to attract him continually to spectacular subjects. Richard Avedon photographed
Jean Shrimpton, a star model of the sixties, in a Mondrian dress.

PAGE 53

One year after the Mondrian dresses, Yves Saint Laurent sent "pop art" down the catwalk. His prototypes are Warhol, Lichtenstein, and Wesselmann. The trendsetter triggered a mass-market fashion with his daring idea, from which the T-shirt industry is still profiting today. Photo by Jean-Claude Sauer.

PAGES 54/55

This photo of Saint Laurent's "pop art" dresses from the fall/winter collection of 1966–67 is a document of the time, a classic illustration of the "swinging sixties"— politically, socially, fashionably, and artistically one of the most exciting decades of the century. The sexual revolution, student revolts, mini-skirts and the astronaut look, the Beatles and Carnaby Street, Andy Warhol and Roy Lichtenstein changed the Western world. Photo by Jean-Claude Sauer.

The sensation of the 1967 fashion summer is Saint Laurent's "Africa" look. His exotic evening dresses of wood and glass beads, of bast and linen, shock the haute couture world, though they are praised by the press as a "fantasy of primitive genius" (Harper's Bazaar). Posing here is Twiggy, one of the idols of the sixties, in a short evening dress trimmed with beads, gold-brown paillettes, and bronze-colored, plastic appliqués. Photo by Bert Stern.

The spring/summer collection of 1968 takes up the African theme once again. Veruschka, the essence of the German "Fräulein Wunder," is playing the Amazon. With black cotton Bermudas and a bronze-ring belt, she's wearing one of the legendary safari shirts that Yves Saint Laurent has made into a fashion classic. Photo by Franco Rubartelli.

PAGES 64/65

The women's tuxedo is a pioneering feat with which Yves Saint Laurent changed fashion. He introduced the first model in 1966; two years later he's showing this daring version with Bermudas and a transparent blouse. The model was a turning point in his work: "I was suddenly aware of the feminine body, I embarked on a dialogue with the feminine and grasped what a modern woman is." Richard Avedon photographed the Bermuda tuxedo on Penelope Tree, a star model of the sixties.

PAGES 66/67

Yves Saint Laurent has collaborated for years with the French sculptor Claude Lalanne. The fashion designer often has the artist create jewelry and accessories. The winter collection of 1969–70 presented an exciting combination of dress and modern sculpture. Claude Lalanne's gold-plated, copper body stockings were united with transparent muslin and evening gowns of archaic Mediterranean splendor. Photo by Manuel Litran.

By 1966 Yves Saint Laurent had opened his first boutique, beginning the production of prêt-à-porter fashion which quickly conquered the world under the trademark "Saint Laurent Rive Gauche." His concept: "Rive Gauche is for the necessities, for the needs of daily life. In haute couture you can allow yourself to dream." Barbara Rix is modeling one of these dresses for her husband, the photographer Jeanloup Sieff.

For the winter of 1970–71, Yves Saint Laurent designs floor-length hearthside dresses of plum blue and black wool-crêpe that are worn with very decorative, printed shawls. Claude Lalanne designed the butterfly jewelry. Photo by Neal Barr.

North Africa is one of the most important and fertile sources of inspiration for Yves Saint Laurent — he has a very personal and profound relationship to this region where he was born. His familiarity with Arabian tradition always leaves its trace in his work. This ash-brown cloth coat from the fall/winter collection of 1970—71 is reminiscent of the magnificent string embroidery on North African djellabas. Photo by David Bailey.

A picture that caused a scandal. "He wanted to shock," recalls Jeanloup Sieff, who took this nude study of Yves Saint Laurent in 1971. The fashion creator, known until now as timid and shy, let his hair down and posed like an apostle for his new men's perfume. The photo caused a stir and made advertising history. It was the first time that a fashion creator had advertised his own perfume.

PAGES 80/81

Ivy tendrils, anemone, and wisteria blossoms twining around the waist—Claude Lalanne is inspired by nature in her bizarrely poetic jewelry creations. She made both of these galvanized gold belts exclusively for Saint Laurent in 1971. Photo by Guy Bourdin.

PAGE 83

Portrait by Hiro during the preparations for the spring/summer collection in 1972. In the mirror, a timeless evening ensemble composed of a floor-length black rep-silk dress, white linen jacket, and a red and white striped muslin blouse.

*A collection that caused shock waves. "Truly hideous," fumed Eugenia Sheppard of
the* International Herald Tribune *when the young Parisian designer displayed the forties
look anew. Brilliant green fox jackets, short pleated skirts, wedge heels, red pouting
mouths, and finger-waves. Women who had worn this wartime fashion themselves rejected
the remake as tasteless and vulgar. "A failure that I can't admit," Saint Laurent later
recalled. But young girls were impressed and copied the forties look, and six months later
Eugenia Sheppard acknowledged her mistake. An accessory with a special twist:
the poppy blossom at the ankle. Photos by Hans Feurer.*

In the summer of 1971 Yves Saint Laurent launched the women's pin-striped suit, another pioneering achievement for sexual equality to follow the women's tuxedo of 1966. "There is no reason for me to dress women differently from men. I don't think a woman is less feminine in pants than in a skirt." Especially when she's wearing this austere manager's suit—of marine blue serge with Bordeaux-colored stripes—with a sheer muslin blouse—also Bordeaux-colored with white dots. Photo by David Bailey.

Marcel Proust is the artist to whom Yves Saint Laurent feels closest. He's constantly designing poetic taffeta gowns in what might be termed "a Proustian vein." A model in the colors of dawn from the fall/winter collection of 1971–72. Photo by Guy Bourdin.

An evening ensemble from the fall/winter collection of 1973–74 that became a classic all its own: the gold and silver–worked, basic gray cardigan is worn with a sand-colored muslin blouse and gray flannel pants. Photo by Helmut Newton.

Yves Saint Laurent is always inventing new variations on his favorite model, the tuxedo.
This austerely cut black gabardine pants suit with a transparent red muslin blouse from the
spring/summer collection of 1974 is inspired by the hotel bellboy. Photo by Guy Bourdin.

"His women aren't just well dressed, they're heroines," says American Vogue. *The woman in this canary yellow crêpe-georgette evening dress from the spring/summer collection of 1976 is more a goddess of revenge than an angel of innocence — cool, beautiful, and slightly perfidious. Photo by Guy Bourdin.*

*Elegance to Saint Laurent is not a question of costly fabrics but rather of allure and a
simplicity that can allow itself some risk now and then. This unassuming black velvet
evening suit from the fall/winter collection of 1974–75 has a bold, dramatic feather collar.
Photo by Francesco Scavullo.*

There was always something confusingly equivocal about women in men's clothing. Never had this ambivalence been better staged than in this photo by Helmut Newton. By 1975 he was already photographing the Saint Laurent suit—like this model in black wool with gray pin-stripes and a pearl gray crêpe-marocain blouse—in that androgynous style that was to become the rage in fashion and show business ten years later.

Red is one of Saint Laurent's favorite colors: "Red is noble — the color of the precious ruby. Red is dangerous, the color of blood and passion. Red is the color of heroines in a battle between life and death." His remarkable sense of color speaks for itself, as he unites this symbolic color with surprising rosy tones like pink and fuchsia. A graceful Far Eastern evening ensemble from the spring/summer collection of 1976. Photo by Guy Bourdin.

PAGES 102/103

Yves Saint Laurent's fall/winter collection of 1976–77 made a lasting change in fashion once again. Sable-trimmed Cossack coats of gold lamé, bright babushka dresses, gold-piped gypsy skirts, luxuriously embroidered boyar-vests, and whisper-thin, glittering blouses with full sleeves, gay country kerchiefs, golden Cossack boots, and opalescent turbans. "A revolution," cheered the International Herald Tribune, "the most dramatic and expensive show ever seen in Paris." The press dubbed this collection "Ballets Russes" in memory of Sergei Diaghilev's Russian ballet troupe that caused a similar sensation in Paris at the beginning of the century. Guy Bourdin photographed three especially magnificent evening ensembles.

PAGES 104/105

Russia on the Seine: Cossack coats of gold brocade, embroidered in jet and trimmed in black mink. A gem from the "Ballets Russes" collection which Duane Michals photographed on the most beautiful bridge in Paris — the Czar Alexander III.

PAGES 106/107

Yves Saint Laurent was pursuing a particular goal with his most expensive collection yet. "It was my answer to the press, which had disqualified the haute couture trade as old-fashioned and antiquated." He not only convinced the press of the artistic worth of luxury fashion, he also brought fantasy back into fashion and triggered a folklore wave that has never completely subsided. Duane Michals arranged a group photo that subtly displays the wide spectrum of combination daytime ensembles in the noble-rustic style of the fall/winter collection of 1976–77.

PAGES 108/109

"I don't know if it's my best collection, but it was certainly my most beautiful," Yves Saint Laurent recalls, casting a retrospective glance at his "Ballets Russes" collection. It was also his most feminine, his most seductive fashion, which Guy Bourdin captured in the Oriental atmosphere of his photo. For the evening gowns shown here, Saint Laurent combined a black velvet bodice with luxurious, wide, moiré and satin skirts.

PAGES 110/111

Snowdon, one of the most refined portrait photographers of our time, immortalized Yves Saint Laurent as a romantic seducer. In his arms he's holding the actress Dayle Haddon, who is wearing a glittering gold evening dress from the legendary "Ballets Russes" collection of 1976—77. The sheep, sculpted by the French artist F.-X. Lalanne, are a part of Saint Laurent's extensive art collection and usually stand in the library of his Paris apartment.

PAGE 112

Barry Lategan effectively sets the scene with the shimmering gold grandeur of old Russia: the long evening ensemble from the fall/winter collection of 1976—77 consists of a violet moiré skirt, black velvet bolero with gold galloons, blouse and fringe stole of colorful, printed muslin-lamé, and an emerald green moiré turban.

PAGE 113

More modest but no less luxurious: Marie Helvin is wearing a long evening dress with a black, jet-embroidered velvet top and a fuchsia faille skirt, also from the fall/winter collection of 1976—77. Photo by Barry Lategan.

A whisper of the Far East with a Spanish touch, from the Rive Gauche collection for spring and summer 1977: kimono coat and stole of printed chintz with an ankle-length satin dress. Photo by Gian Paolo Barbieri.

Black transparent muslin with gold dots and black-gold silk organza worked into a stunning evening ensemble from the fall/winter collection of 1977–78. Photo by Lothar Schmid.

Imperial China was the inspiration for the fall/winter collection of 1977–78. The splendid suits of the Chinese court, the opulence of its brocades and silks, moved Yves Saint Laurent to more creative fireworks. An evening ensemble consisting of a black, blue, and gold brocade coat with mink hood and piping, blue satin pants, and high-cut, fur-trimmed boots along with gold leather gloves. Photo by Lothar Schmid.

From the same collection: a black, gold, and violet striped, damask-lamé evening ensemble to go along with a jacket decorated in tassels and fringe, and long, narrow, black-lacquered satin pants. Photo by Lothar Schmid.

A particularly exquisite variation from the China collection of 1977–78: a mink-cuffed gold damask overcoat in expressive relief— the fabric was so precious that Saint Laurent's tailor had hesitations about cutting into it— and quilted black velvet pants. Photo by Lothar Schmid.

The world is indebted to Yves Saint Laurent's flirtation with ancient China for one other luxury product: "Opium," launched in the fall of 1977, became one of the most successful perfumes. It influenced the entire fragrance industry with its heavy, exotic note.

As early as 1960–61, Yves Saint Laurent made these evening dresses, inspired by Goya, at Dior for the fall/winter collection. An off-the-shoulder gown of strass-studded, black-dotted chiffon with a black velvet stole (left); on the right, an opalescent satin dress shimmers through black embroidered tulle. Photo by William Klein.

On the opposite page is a model from the Rive Gauche collection of spring/summer 1978 inspired by one of these early designs, a low-necked, black cotton, lace-up bodice of obvious Spanish origin. Photo by Helmut Newton.

In the fall/winter collection of 1981—82, Saint Laurent presented the tuxedo in suit form with a short and a long skirt. Photo by Helmut Newton.

PAGE 149

*A three-piece daytime ensemble from the Rive Gauche collection of fall/winter 1981—82: a violet fabric cape with velvet piping complements the plum blue, wool-crêpe tunic embroidered with beads and paillettes, a straight-cut, knee-length skirt of ruby red silk velour, and the indispensable small velvet cap — in this picture, caramel brown.
Photo by Denis Piel.*

PAGES 150/151

A piquant mix: the simple, timeless tunic in marine blue jersey and a gold-colored leather skirt. Helmut Newton photographed this ensemble from the Rive Gauche collection for fall/winter of 1981—82 on Violetta in a classical setting.

A vision by Helmut Newton, who, like a film director, staged this austere tailored suit with an elegant silver fox boa, from the fall/winter collection of 1981–82.

For the fall/winter collection of 1959–60 at Dior, Saint Laurent designed this black taffeta cocktail dress. Photo by Irving Penn.

Twenty-two years later, in the fall/winter collection of 1981–82, he takes up the basic pattern again for a short, hot pink taffeta dress. Photo by Roland Bianchini.

PAGES 156/157

Yves Saint Laurent lives out his love for the theater in haute couture. At the presentation of the fall/winter collection of 1981–82, the bride wore — almost — black: a dramatic gown of dark violet, almost black, rep-silk. And Mounia, a favorite model and muse of the master for years, looked like a fairy-tale princess under her black tulle veil. The flower children also wore Yves Saint Laurent creations of plum blue rep-silk and velvet.
Photo by Arthur Elgort.

PAGES 158/159

These two romantic models from the Rive Gauche collection for fall/winter of 1981–82 tell tales of the glamorous life in dream castles. On the left is a daytime ensemble with a wide bronze-colored cloth cape, a long jacquard sweater, and green velvet skirt; on the right, an evening dress of iridescent black taffeta and black lace. Photo by Helmut Newton.

PAGE 161

This long evening sheath of black velvet with its graceful, billowing Persian blue satin cape is a model from the fall/winter collection of 1982–83. It was expressively staged by Bruce Weber, one of the most important American fashion photographers of the younger generation.

PAGE 163

This Rive Gauche model from the spring/summer collection of 1982 is reminiscent of the transparent look of the sixties — the black taffeta topcoat goes with a knee-length sleeveless dress and black lace T-shirt top. Photo by François Lamy.

PAGE 164

This long evening dress of black velvet and white silk-crêpe comes from the fall/winter collection of 1982–83. Horst imbues the scene with timeless thirties elegance by his dramatic lighting effects.

PAGE 165

"The most important thing about a dress is the material — that is, the fabric and the color,"
Yves Saint Laurent said in an interview with Le Monde. *Here is an example, an*
evening dress of borage blue satin and black velvet (fall/winter of 1982–83). Photo by Horst.

Red and black, a classic combination that Yves Saint Laurent loves, presented here in a coatdress from the Rive Gauche collection of spring/summer 1983. Photo by Roxanne Lowit.

Rococo and classicism worked together in breathtaking unison in this model from the fall/winter collection of 1982–83. The long-sleeved, sophisticatedly simple sheath of black velvet offers an overwhelming back view: a little silk taffeta tail, and a huge bow in iridescent colors of the rising sun. Photo by Antonio Guccione.

*The feline suppleness of Amalia's exotic beauty is exceptionally well emphasized by the
leopard pattern of a pure silk evening dress from the fall/winter collection of 1982—83.
Photo by Helmut Newton.*

Insights – This afternoon dress of black and red printed silk damask with its waist-deep neckline from the fall/winter collection of 1983–84 was photographed by David Seidner through the door of an old Parisian house.

*Saint Laurent combined white satin and black velvet in the fall/winter collection of 1983—84
to make a small party dress with a knee-length balloon skirt, reminiscent of the figures in the
Italian commedia dell'arte. Photo by Frank Horvat.*

Saint Laurent's perfectionism is one of the reasons for his unusually long and unchallenged reign in the fast-paced fashion world. In 1982, after twenty years of high-powered career, he confessed in an interview: "I'm no longer concerned with sensation and innovation, but with the perfection of my style." A convincing example is this suit of black grain de poudre from the spring/summer collection of 1983. Photo by Sacha.

The Arsenale, Venice's old military harbor, creates the grandiose backdrop for a noble evening gown — black velvet tunic over black silk-crêpe skirt — from the fall/winter collection of 1983—84. The staging, a mixture of eroticism, pathos, and irony, carries the unmistakable signature of Helmut Newton.

For the perfectionist Yves Saint Laurent, the paintings of Piet Mondrian are the quintessence
of stylistic purity. Duane Michals portrays the private Saint Laurent, standing before a
Mondrian and a Chinese sculpture. Photo from 1983.

The young American photographer David Seidner has given fashion photography of
the eighties a highly artificial and poetic direction. With the instinct of a sculptor, he imbues
the fabric of these dream gowns with a sensuous plasticity. An evening ensemble – a
luxurious, wide coat of yellow China rep-silk with a long black velvet and lace sheath
(fall/winter of 1983–84).

Yves Saint Laurent creations are an invitation to play games with mirror images. David Seidner has a fine sense for the narcissistic element in fashion. This black velvet knee-length sheath, draped most decoratively with pink taffeta, comes from the fall/winter collection of 1983—84.

Yves Saint Laurent with a model from the fall/winter collection of 1983—84, the famous long evening dress of black velvet with gigantic rose-colored satin bows. Photo by David Bailey.

On the right, the back view of the same dress — a photo by Gilles Tapie that became a classic.

PAGE 187

A favorite theme of Yves Saint Laurent, playing through the red palette in all imaginable nuances. This festive shantung dress from the Rive Gauche collection of spring/summer 1984 was remarkable for its brilliant composition of rose, pink, tomato, fuchsia—and violet for the shoes. Photo by David Seidner.

PAGES 188/189

These mirror images conceptualized as a diptych by David Seidner bring out the extravagant hats of two models from the spring/summer collection of 1985: on the left, a headdress of bright cock feathers with a white crêpe dress; on the right, a black, broad-brimmed hat with white dots worn with a steel gray whipcord suit and a black and white patterned blouse. Hats are the crown of every couture creation for Yves Saint Laurent; he is one of the few designers who still maintain their own hat ateliers.

Once again, Helmut Newton; once again, Venice: a daytime ensemble from the Rive Gauche collection of fall/winter 1983–84, consisting of a red jersey tunic over a black knee-length skirt along with a gondolier hat of red panama.

A long, narrowly cut evening dress of black crêpe marocain with violet,
green, and fuchsia silk sashes, in 1984. Photo by Dominique Issermann.

For the Rive Gauche collection of spring/summer 1984, Saint Laurent designed a pink jersey tunic with matching turban and a mustard skirt. Photo by Jeanloup Sieff.

The accessories, which Saint Laurent insists on putting together himself, play a decisive role in the interplay of individual elements in a creation. Here, the black-dotted gloves reaching to the upper arm and a pink-colored toque spice this festive short evening dress of black tulle and white moiré with velvet appliqués. 1984. Photo by Gilles Tapie.

A model with grandeur: the long evening dress from the spring/summer collection of 1984
combines black lace and coral organza. Another important accessory here is the dotted gloves.
Photo by Peter Lindbergh.

This opulent evening coat of silk in blue cameo tones and black velvet reveals Saint Laurent's theatrical talent. A creation from the fall/winter collection of 1984—85. Photo by Norman Parkinson.

PAGES 202/203

The long white satin evening dress from the fall/winter collection of 1984—85 was staged on a bronze sculpture by Maillol, photographed by Norman Parkinson. A photo in which pathos and humor blend in daring unison.

203

This model from the Rive Gauche collection of fall/winter 1984—85 is characterized by the sparkling jeweled buttons and huge wine-red taffeta sash that give the "little black one" wit and sex appeal. Photo by Guy Bourdin.

A dress of red sateen from the Rive Gauche collection of spring/summer 1985.
Photo by Helmut Newton.

From the Rive Gauche collection of spring/summer 1985: a combination of black and turquoise silk jersey with a broad-rimmed hat of black panama and sheer horsehair net. On the wall is a portrait of Yves Saint Laurent by Andy Warhol, done in 1972. Photo by Helmut Newton.

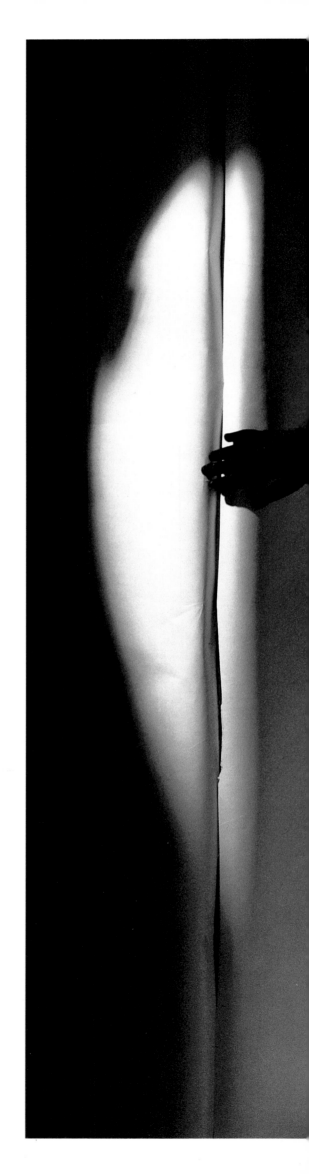

This short black wool-crêpe dress with the shoulders asymmetrically draped in red satin comes from the fall/winter collection of 1986–87. Photo by Horst.

The black velvet and flame red satin evening dress was the highlight of the fall/winter collection of 1985–86. This photograph by David Seidner articulates the poetry of the black-red contrast brilliantly.

The long evening dress of spring green silk for the wide skirt and black guipure embroidery comes from the spring/summer collection of 1986. Photo by David Seidner.

The highly praised spring/summer collection of 1988 was spectacular as seldom before, and showcased rich, gay paillettes embroideries after paintings by Van Gogh, Matisse, and the French cubists. Here is an elegant evening cape embroidered with a motif after Georges Braque. Photo by Irving Penn.

Biography

1936 Yves Saint Laurent is born on August 1, in Oran, Algeria. "Oran was our world at that time. It wasn't Algiers, the metaphysical city of Camus, yielding white truths. Nor was it Marrakesh, with its balmy, roseate magic. Oran: a melting pot of traders from everywhere — and most of all from somewhere else; a glittering, multicolored patchwork of a city, under the steady North African sun" (Yves Saint Laurent, 1983).

1947 At the age of eleven he attends a performance of Molière's *L'Ecole des Femmes*, directed by Louis Jouvet. So struck is he by Christian Bérard's scenery and costumes, that he amuses himself by making a model of them. This passion for the theater is never to leave him.

1953 Yves Saint Laurent takes first prize in a competition sponsored by the Secrétariat International de la Laine for a cocktail dress with an asymmetrical neckline, later to be worked out by Hubert de Givenchy.

1954 At the age of seventeen he goes to Paris to learn to be a couturier, spending three months at the Ecole de la Chambre Syndicale de la Haute Couture. It is during this period that he begins corresponding with Michel de Brunhoff, the publisher of French *Vogue*, who discovers the young designer's talent: "Dear Sir, I find your designs most interesting, and can only repeat what I told you when you were in Paris, that your gift for fashion is beyond doubt. I have marked with a cross those of your designs that I consider the most successful. If I were you, I would take advantage of this year when you are relatively free of other commitments to work as much as possible from nature — landscape, still life and portraits, as well as fashion models. As a matter of fact, I am rather afraid that your particular talents do not encourage you to work hard enough on your drawing. I can see that you are still influenced by Bérard. All to the good — he was one of my oldest friends, and you could not choose a better master. But I should tell you that he did work hard at his drawing, and the few wonderful portraits he left behind him — remarkable portraits — are inclined to make one sorry that he devoted the end of his life solely to scenery and costume for the theater, and to fashion ..." (Letter from Michel de Brunhoff to Yves Saint Laurent, February 24, 1954).

"Dear Sir, I am sorry not to have answered you earlier, but I wanted to wait for the results of my examination before doing so. As I had hoped, they proved entirely satisfactory, and I am to move to Paris at the beginning of the fall. Perhaps my plans are a little too ambitious. Like Bérard, I want to focus on a number of different activities, which are really all parts of one thing — that is, scenery, costumes, decoration, and illustration for the theater. On the other hand, I am very much drawn to fashion. No doubt my career will develop naturally out of one or the other of these areas. In any case, do you still think I should start by attending the Chambre Syndicale de la Couture? If you think otherwise, I should be grateful if you would tell me. As you recommended, I am doing a lot of painting, but I am also continuing to design theater sets and costumes, as well as dresses, which I will send you soon..." (Letter from Yves Saint Laurent to Michel de Brunhoff, summer, 1954). Michel de Brunhoff is struck by the resemblance of Yves Saint Laurent's sketches to Christian Dior's forthcoming collection — the "Ligne A." He introduces him to Dior, who immediately hires him as his assistant and principal associate. "Working with Christian Dior was a miracle for me. My admiration for him knew no bounds. He had created a fashion house that was unique by surrounding himself with exceptional people. He was an extraordinary master, who taught me the fundamentals of my art. I owe a large part of my life to him, and whatever happens, I will never forget the years spent at his side" (Yves Saint Laurent, 1983).

1957　After Christian Dior's death, on November 15, Yves Saint Laurent is appointed his successor. "After the death of Christian Dior, the opportunity to create my own collections led me to abandon my plan of working for the theater. At the age of twenty-one I entered a sort of citadel of fame, which was to trap me for the rest of my life. I would never lose my love for the theater, but in the meantime Dior had taught me to cherish something beyond fashion and style: the essential nobility of the couturier's work. I maintain that the designer who cannot also call himself a couturier, who has never mastered the subtlest intricacies of the actual putting together of his creations, is like a sculptor who hands over his designs to some artisan to work out. This sort of truncated method of working is akin to an interrupted act of love — the result inescapably impoverished and flawed" (Yves Saint Laurent, 1983).

1958　On January 30 he presents his first collection, the "Ligne Trapèze," and gains instant renown. It is on this day that he meets Pierre Bergé.

1959　For the first time, Yves Saint Laurent designs theater costumes — for Roland Petit's production of the ballet *Cyrano de Bergerac* at the Théâtre de l'Alhambra in Paris.

1960　His fall/winter collection is the subject of much discussion by a public and press amazed to see turtleneck sweaters and leather jackets, directly inspired by street fashion.
In September he is drafted into military service. Marc Bohan takes his place at Christian Dior.

1961　His contract with Christian Dior now broken, Yves Saint Laurent decides to set up his own fashion house, in association with Pierre Bergé, and in September he moves to a two-room apartment in rue La Boétie, Paris.
At the same time, he designs scenery and costumes for Roland Petit's ballet *Les Forains* and for the "Spectacle Zizi Jeanmaire" at the Théâtre de l'Alhambra.

1962　On January 29, Yves Saint Laurent presents his first collection in the former townhouse of the painter Forain, rue Spontini. The press is ecstatic: "The best collection of suits since Chanel," writes *Life* magazine, and from Dino Buzzati in *Corriere della Sera*: "This was perhaps the most eagerly anticipated of the collections, all the more so since it marked the end of the year's great parade of elegance. This shy young dauphin of haute couture, a former pupil of Christian Dior, has just opened his own fashion house, and this morning he subjected the first creations bearing his mark to the judgment of the inner circle. 'Things are happening exactly as the Americans predicted,' comments an expert. 'This year they were betting on the new generation, and they won.' Concluding the show, a white piqué quilted wedding dress provoked an ovation from the public. Then the pale face of the young couturier appeared for an instant in the wings — an instant only, before he was surrounded by a surge of admirers, and embraced and devoured...."
The same year, Yves Saint Laurent designs the scenery and costumes for Roland Petit's *Les Chants de Maldoror* and *Rhapsodie Espagnole* at the Théâtre National de Paris. He continues his work for the theater with the scenery and costumes for the "Spectacle Zizi Jeanmaire," also at the Théâtre National de Paris (1963), and the costumes for the Renaud-Barrault production of *The Marriage of Figaro* and *Il faut passer par les Nuages* (1964).

1964　The spring/summer collection is badly received by the press. Some years later in an interview with *Paris Match*, Yves Saint Laurent explains: "Personally, I have never been able to work with a wooden mannequin; I like to play with fabric, unfurling it onto the model (I need a model who inspires me), wrapping it around her, making it move until the dress or suit clicks into shape.... My only failed collection – a complete fiasco (1964, the year of Courrèges' first success) – I had no good models, no inspiration" (Yves Saint Laurent, *Paris Match*, 1981).

1965　Diana Vreeland is enraptured by the spring/summer collection, which she declares "ravishing, subtle, polished. French, and very feminine" (American *Vogue*, April 1965). The fall/winter "Ligne Mondrian" constitutes a landmark in Yves Saint Laurent's sources of inspiration. "Abstraction as the rule. Clothing for tomorrow. Severe lines in white jersey, perfectly proportioned to flatter the figure" (*Harper's Bazaar*, September 1965). Contemporary art will influence him ever more deeply over the course of his career. "Contrary to what one might think, the severe lines of Mondrian's pictures worked well on the female form; shoes were low-heeled with silver buckles, and I shortened the dresses dramatically. The result provoked a sensation" (Yves Saint Laurent, *Paris Match*, 1981). Still working for the theater, Yves Saint Laurent designs the costumes for Roland Petit's *Adage et Variations* and *Notre Dame de Paris* at the Théâtre National de l'Opéra, as well as for *Des Journées Entières Dans les Arbres* by Marguerite Duras, with Madeleine Renaud, at the Théâtre de l'Odéon.

1966　The first tuxedos for women appear in the fall/winter collection, as well as "pop art" dresses, inspired by current artistic trends and by Andy Warhol in particular. "If I had to choose a piece among every one that I have ever shown, it would be, without a shadow of doubt, the tuxedo. It appeared for the first time in 1966, with a transparent blouse and men's trousers, and has been a part of my collection ever since. In a way, it is a sort of Yves Saint Laurent 'label' " (Yves Saint Laurent, *Paris Match*, 1981).
On September 26, the first ready-to-wear boutique opens – Saint Laurent Rive Gauche, at 21 rue de Tournon, Paris (later it moved to 6 Place Saint Sulpice). It was the first in a long chain throughout the world.
Yves Saint Laurent designs the costumes for Arletty in Jean Cocteau's *Les Monstres Sacrés* at the *Théâtre des Ambassadeurs*.

1967　The spring/summer collection draws its inspiration from primitive art and African dress. Yves Saint Laurent designs the costumes for the Renaud-Barrault production of Edward Albee's *A Delicate Balance*. He also dresses Catherine Deneuve for Luis Buñuel's *Belle de Jour*.
Editions Tchou publishes *La Vilaine Lulu*, illustrated by Yves Saint Laurent.

1968　The spring/summer collection brings the "Safari Look," with the first safari jacket (he will create a masculine version of this in 1969). It also brings transparent fabrics and the jumpsuit – the latter to be successfully revived in 1984.
Two galleries, one in New York, the other in London, exhibit his designs for the theater.

1969　The first mini-dresses for evening and the first man's suit appear. The latter becomes a leitmotiv of Yves Saint Laurent's work, as he adapts this traditionally masculine garment for the dynamic woman in a modern world. "I have been strongly influenced by a photograph of Marlene Dietrich in a man's suit. A woman who dresses like a man – in tuxedo, blazer or sailor suit – has to be infinitely feminine in order to wear clothes which were not meant for her. She must be pretty and refined down to the smallest detail" (Yves Saint Laurent, American *Vogue*, 1983).

Yves Saint Laurent designs Catherine Deneuve's wardrobe for François Truffaut's film *La Sirène du Mississippi* and in 1970 he designs the costumes for the "Revue Zizi Jeanmaire" in the Casino de Paris, and for "Sylvie Vartan" at the Olympia.

1971   The spring/summer collection — the so-called Collection 40 — provokes a scandalized outcry. Yves Saint Laurent explains that he was reacting against fashion's current direction: "That collection, which the world labeled kitsch, was a reaction against the absurd turn that fashion had taken... with its 'gypsies' bedecked in bracelets and trailing long, flowing skirts. I conceived my collection as a sort of humorous protest, and the world has taken it seriously. After this parenthesis, returning to my own real style, I feel much surer of myself" (Yves Saint Laurent, 1972).

The same year, Yves Saint Laurent designs the scenery and costumes for the "Spectacle Johnny Halliday" at the Palais des Sports.

1972   "The Yves Saint Laurent collection has given fashion a shot in the arm in the midst of this wonderful European spring. The man is still, simply, the greatest couturier in the world, and this season has given us his best collection in many years" (*Harper's Bazaar*, 1972). In the fall, Nina Hyde declares in the Washington *Post* that "Yves Saint Laurent has changed the face, and perhaps the future, of fashion."

Yves Saint Laurent again designs costumes for the "Revue Zizi Jeanmaire" at the Casino de Paris, and for "Sylvie Vartan" at the Olympia.

Andy Warhol paints his famous series of portraits of Yves Saint Laurent.

1973   A year devoted to the theater. Yves Saint Laurent designs the costumes for Maya Plisetskaya in *La Rose Malade* with music by Gustav Mahler. He also creates the costumes for Madeleine Renaud in *Harold and Maude* by Colin Higgins, for Jeanne Moreau, Delphine Seyrig, and Gerard Depardieu in Peter Handke's *La Chevauchée sur le Lac de Constance* and for Roland Petit's ballet *Schéhérazade* with music by Maurice Ravel.

1974   The Galerie Proscenium in Paris exhibits Yves Saint Laurent's set designs and theater costumes.

In the same year, he dresses Anny Duperey for Alain Resnais' film *L'Affaire Stavisky*. In July the Maison de Couture is installed in 5 Avenue Marceau, in a townhouse dating from the Second Empire.

1975   The spring/summer collection presents "narrow little dresses, simple and easy to wear, which is why women are turning back to the dress" (American *Vogue*, March 1975).

1976   Yves Saint Laurent presents his famous "Opéra/Ballets Russes" collection, which enjoys exceptional success internationally, and makes the front page of *The New York Times*: "A revolutionary collection, which will alter the course of world fashion."

"In his latest collection, Yves Saint Laurent has managed to remind us that fashion at its ultimate, as evinced by haute couture, becomes costume. Here we can see just how sophisticated fashion has become in its interpretation of history, reflecting a nostalgia not for the past, but for that eternal present which lies beyond the past" (Pierre Schneider, American *Vogue*, September 1976).

"I do not know whether it is my best collection, but it is my most beautiful" (Yves Saint Laurent, 1976).

Yves Saint Laurent designs Ellen Burstyn's costumes for Alain Renais' film *Providence*.

1977 The collection draws its inspiration from Spain, with dresses reminiscent of Velasquez. In the fall collection, at the time the perfume "Opium" is launched, the spirit of the Orient (a part of the world which still fascinates Yves Saint Laurent) prevails. "It was a profoundly egocentric show! I returned to the age of ease and elegance, in some ways delving into my own past, with references to favorite operas and painters. It was theater! But it was also all that is hidden in the innermost depths of my soul.

"I belong to a world devoted to elegance. I grew up in a world much attached to tradition, yet at the same time, I wanted to change all that. I felt myself drawn to the past, while the future drove me ahead. I feel divided, and I think I always will be, for I am familiar with one world, yet am aware of the presence of the other" (Yves Saint Laurent, 1977).

He designs new costumes for the "Revue Zizi Jeanmaire" at the Théâtre Bobino.

1978 The Galerie Proscenium mounts a second exhibition of his theater design. He has just created the scenery and costumes for Jean Cocteau's *l'Aigle à Deux Têtes* at the Théâtre de l'Athénée-Louis Jouvet, and the costumes for Ingrid Caven's show at Cabaret Le Pigalle. Eighteen years since his turtlenecks and leather jackets made a sensation, Yves Saint Laurent shows in his fall/winter collection that he is still much influenced by street fashion. "This collection is very elegant — provocative, yet also completely modern, a combination which might appear contradictory. My aim was purity, but then I added some unexpected extras: pointed collars, little hats, shoes with pompoms. It was like winking — lending a little humor to haute couture, adapting the gimmicks of street fashion to suit its tone, introducing the air of freedom of the streets — the arrogance and provocation of punk, for example. All this, of course, with dignity, luxury, and style" (Yves Saint Laurent, 1978).

He writes the preface to Nancy Hall-Duncan's *Histoire de la Photographie de Mode*, published by Editions du Chêne.

1979 Before the opening of a big exhibition in Paris of Picasso's work, Yves Saint Laurent dedicates his fall/winter collection to the painter, with embroidered dresses inspired by the pictures.

1980 The fall/winter collection is devoted to literature and poetry, with references to Apollinaire, Aragon, and Cocteau. He calls it his "Collection Shakespeare."

Yves Saint Laurent designs the scenery and costumes for *Cher Monsieur*, a play by Jerome Kelly, adapted by Jean Cocteau, at the Théâtre de l'Athénée-Louis Jouvet, with Edwige Feuillere and Jean Marais.

1981 The fall/winter collection reintroduces the great classics. It is also dedicated to Matisse. "Like Chanel, I have come to the firm conclusion that 'good things never go out of fashion.' I opened my first collection with a pea coat, and I am closing this year's with a pea coat. There is a basis to my collection which goes back twenty years: the blazer, the pea coat, the smock, the raincoat (in 1965 I was the first to bring out black vinyl raincoats), the pants suit, the blouse, the safari jacket and the tuxedo which allows women the same freedom of movement as men" (Yves Saint Laurent, *Paris Match*, December 1981).

Yves Saint Laurent creates a special uniform for Marguerite Yourcenar, the first woman to be admitted to the Académie Française.

1982 Yves Saint Laurent celebrates the twentieth anniversary of his fashion house at the Lido, where Diana Vreeland personally presents him with the International Fashion Award of the Council of Fashion Designers of America.

1983 The *Dictionnaire Larousse* adds Yves Saint Laurent's name to its pages.

Diana Vreeland organizes a large retrospective at the Metropolitan Museum of Art in New York: "Yves Saint Laurent, Twenty-Five Years of Design." It is the first time a show has been devoted to a living designer. "Yves Saint Laurent has established a place for himself in the history of fashion which will last for many years. His twenty-six years of creation show that he manages to thrill the public with every one of his annual collections. What a great career!" (Diana Vreeland, *Time*, December 1983).

"After many years of exploration, my art continues to fascinate me. I can think of nothing more exciting. You think you have reached the limit, that things have come to a halt, that you are finished forever, when suddenly vast perspectives emerge, of the sort which you had thought beyond your reach — possible now because of what you have done before. So many times have I felt myself powerless, shattered, in despair, confronted by the black curtain of depression. Yet so many times this curtain has torn apart, leaving an opening through which limitless horizons stretch ahead, offering me my greatest moments of joy, and, I must add, moments of real pride" (Yves Saint Laurent, 1983).

Yves Saint Laurent designs the costumes for *Savannah Bay* by Marguerite Duras at the Théâtre du Rond Point.

1985 While the spring/summer collection is once more inspired by Africa, a second retrospective is mounted in China, at the Palace of Fine Arts in Beijing: "Yves Saint Laurent, 1958–1985."

President François Mitterand personally presents him with the medal of the Chevalier de la légion d'Honneur at the Elysée palace.

He receives an Oscar as the greatest couturier for his entire oeuvre at the Paris Opéra.

1986 An important retrospective is put on at the Musée des Arts de la Mode: "Yves Saint Laurent, 28 Years of Design," while the Musée des Arts Décoratifs exhibits his theater design. "His life is a legend. His name is an empire in itself. His dresses, still haunted by the scent of the women who loved them, find a place in our museums. He himself transcends all of this — the glory, the tributes, the clamor and the tumult — with the distant silence of a great Proustian dandy ..." (Bernard-Henry Lévy in his preface to the book *Yves Saint Laurent*, published by Editions Herscher in 1986).

In November he is appointed Chief Consultant to the government of the People's Republic of China.

At the same time, Yves Saint Laurent and Pierre Bergé, with the help of financier Carlo de Benedetti, buy back the Charles of the Ritz group, which includes Yves Saint Laurent perfumes.

The exhibition "Yves Saint Laurent, 28 Years of Design" takes place in Moscow.

1987 The same show is put on in the throne room of the Hermitage in Leningrad, before going on to the Gallery of New South Wales in Sydney, Australia.

1988 The spring/summer collection is a homage to Cubism, brilliantly conveyed by means of faces, doves and guitars, and also incorporating Van Gogh's irises and sunflowers. "To set in motion what is static on a woman's body" (Yves Saint Laurent, *Paris Match*, February 1988).

Still life with hats, photographed by Bettina Rheims in Yves Saint Laurent's haute couture salon in Avenue Marceau, Paris, 1982.

PHOTO CREDITS